JBIOG
Brown
Streissguth, Tom

John Brown

John Brown

by Tom Streissguth
illustrations by Ralph L. Ramstad

Carolrhoda Books, Inc./Minneapolis

Editor's note: In John Brown's time, the town of Harpers
Ferry, West Virginia, was known as Harper's Ferry. The town
of Charles Town, West Virginia, was known as Charlestown.
Both Harper's Ferry and Charlestown were part of the state
of Virginia until 1863, when the state of West Virginia was created.

The publisher wishes to thank Jim Stewart, professor of history at
Macalester College, for his invaluable assistance in reviewing the
manuscript.

The photograph on page 46 appears courtesy of the Boston Athenaeum.

Carolrhoda Books, Inc., c/o The Lerner Publishing Group
241 First Avenue North, Minneapolis, MN 55401 U.S.A.

Website address: www.lernerbooks.com

Library of Congress Cataloging-in-Publication Data

Streissguth, Thomas, 1958–
    John Brown / by Tom Streissguth ; illustrations by Ralph Ramstad.
        p. cm. — (Carolrhoda on my own books)
      Summary: A brief biography of the man who fought against slavery
    in the Kansas Territory and who led a revolt at Harper's Ferry in 1859.
      ISBN 1-57505-334-9
      1. Brown, John, 1800–1859—Juvenile literature. 2. Abolitionists—
    United States—Biography—Juvenile literature. [1. Brown, John,
    1800–1859. 2. Abolitionists.] I. Ramstad, Ralph L., 1919– ill.
    II. Title. III. Series.
    E451.S89 1999
    973.7'.116'092—dc21   99-29732
    [B]

Manufactured in the United States of America
1 2 3 4 5 6 – JR – 04 03 02 01 00 99

To Harry Lerner, with my congratulations
on book publishing well done.
—T. S.

To my wife, Ruth, and our children of the
electronic age. They brought me to the
Internet with its wealth of information,
which was certainly required for John Brown!
—R. L. R.

Hudson Township, Ohio
1812

Twelve-year-old John Brown
drove the cattle along a forest path.
He had walked almost a hundred miles.
The cattle were his only company.
John was taking them to market
for his father, Owen.
John wanted to do a good job
to make his father proud.

Owen Brown was strict.

He worked hard in his tannery

with John and his other sons,

making leather.

Owen believed every word of the Bible.
He punished his children
for breaking rules.
He also taught them
that slavery was wrong.

Many people in the United States
owned slaves.
The slaves had been brought from Africa.
White people bought and sold them
like houses or cattle.
Even the slaves' children could be sold.

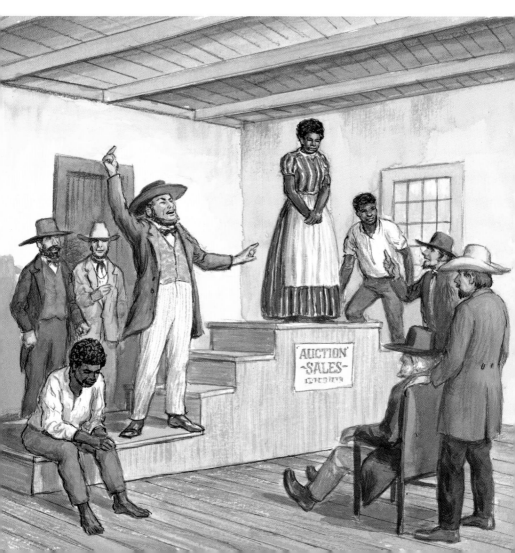

Most slaves worked in the South.

Many lived in shacks.

They could not own anything.

The laws in the South

did not protect the slaves.

Their owners could beat them.

Slaves who ran away were whipped.

Once, when John brought
Owen's cattle to market,
he made friends with a young slave.
The boy wore rags.
He looked hungry.

John saw the boy's owner
beat him with a shovel.
John never forgot that boy.
Like Owen Brown, John hated slavery.
People who wanted slavery to end
were called abolitionists.
Those who believed in it
were said to be proslavery.

When John grew up, he left home.
He married and raised a family.
He was as strict as Owen Brown.
His children worked hard
in the tannery John owned.
John taught them to live by the Bible
and to hate slavery.

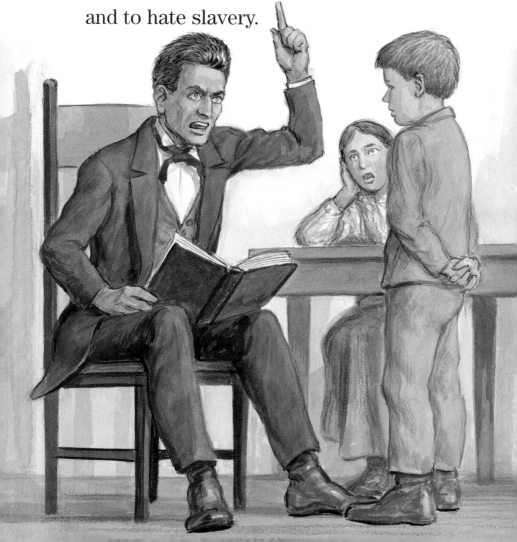

John spoke out often against slavery.
He believed that God wanted him
to free the slaves.
He spoke long and loud
in churches and at meetings.
Many people listened
to his strong words and booming voice.

But John believed
that talking was not enough.
He came up with a secret plan.
He would send guns and swords
to some of the slaves.
John hoped the slaves
would attack their owners,
then run away.

John would help the slaves hide
in the Appalachian Mountains.
Some would go to Canada.
Slavery was against the law there.
Others would stay behind and fight.
They would frighten the owners.
Then the owners would free their slaves.
Finally, John thought,
slavery would end.

John told his plan

to a man named Frederick Douglass.

Douglass had once been a slave.

Then he had run away.

He was famous for writing

and speaking against slavery.

At first, Douglass believed that slavery

could end without fighting.

Writers and ministers could tell people

why slavery was wrong.

The government might

pass laws against it.

But John was sure that words alone

would never free the slaves.

They would have to fight.

After talking with John,

Douglass began to agree.

As John got older,
people grew angrier about slavery.
Many Southerners said
they needed the work of slaves.
Many Northerners believed
it was wrong to own people.

18

In 1854, five of John's sons
decided to leave Ohio.
They walked and rode
a thousand miles west
to the Kansas Territory.
The land in Kansas was good.
Wheat and corn grew tall there.
Cattle and sheep grew fat
in the green fields.

Soon Kansas would become a state.

Would slavery be allowed there?

The people of Kansas

would vote to decide.

Only the white men

who lived in Kansas could vote.

Slaves and women could not.

Abolitionists and proslavery men

rushed to Kansas.

The proslavery voters won.

Kansas abolitionists were angry.

John's sons thought the two sides

might go to war.

They asked for John's help.

John and his family were very poor.

He had not been able

to put his plan into action.

John believed that a war in Kansas
would help him free slaves.
He soon left Ohio
with a wagon full of guns.

Kansas Territory

1855

John joined his five sons.

They met many other abolitionists.

Soon John became one of their leaders.

More proslavery men came to Kansas
to start farms of their own.

The two groups lived side by side.

Each group grew angrier over slavery.

One night, a man brought news.

Proslavery men had attacked Lawrence,

an abolitionist town.

Fires were burning

on the town's main street.

John listened.

His eyes and his voice

grew sharp with anger.

He asked for help.

Who would join him?

John and seven men set out.

They hid near a place

where proslavery families lived.

The next night,

John's group killed five men.

John Brown had said
he would do anything to end slavery.
He was even willing to kill.
After that night,
abolitionists and proslavery men
fought in Kansas for weeks.
Many people on both sides died.

Hundreds of men hunted
John and his sons.
John had to leave Kansas.
But his fight was not over.
Slavery still split the country.
Soon, John believed, war would come.

John returned east
to ask his friends
for more money and guns.
He made a new plan.
He would take men
to the town of Harper's Ferry, Virginia.
Many guns were stored there.

John and his group
would steal the guns.
John's men would spread the news.
John hoped that slaves
would run away to join him.
He hoped abolitionists would come, too.
John would give them the guns.
The war to end slavery would begin.

John was sure his plan would work.

Again, he told the plan

to Frederick Douglass.

He wanted Douglass to help him.

Douglass thought the plan was brave.

But he also thought it would not work.

Many people would be killed,

and slavery would not end.

John did not agree.

To free the slaves, he said,

there would have to be fighting.

There would probably be a war.

Harper's Ferry, Virginia
October 16, 1859

Night had fallen.

John and a group of over twenty men
set out on a dusty road.

John's sons Oliver and Watson
had joined him.

The group crossed the Potomac River.

They marched quietly into town.

John's men took several prisoners.
They broke into the building
where the guns were kept.
Then they waited for morning.
John sent a few men
to find slaves to join them.

Word spread quickly.
Townspeople began shooting
at John and his men.
They fired back.
The fighting went on all day and night.
John was sure that an army of slaves
would arrive soon.
But the next morning,
soldiers reached the town.

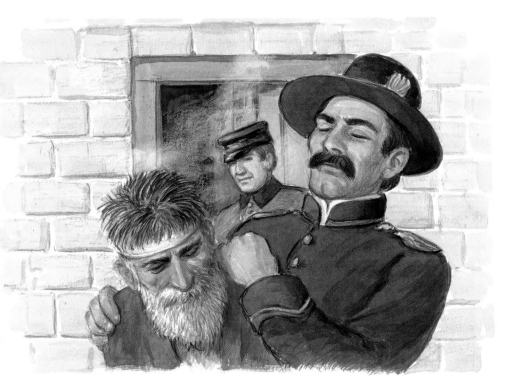

John Brown and his men were caught.

They had killed seven people.

John's two sons

and eight of his other men also died.

Only five of his men got away.

No army of slaves had come to help.

Most slaves were too far away.

They didn't know what John had done.

The Harper's Ferry plan had failed.

John Brown and four of his men
sat in jail in Charlestown, Virginia.
John was put on trial quickly.
Many white people in the South
were afraid of a slave attack.
They wanted John to be hanged.

All over the country,
people read and heard about the trial.
Hundreds of people came to watch.
John lay on a cot, facing the judge.
His face showed cuts
from the fight at Harper's Ferry.

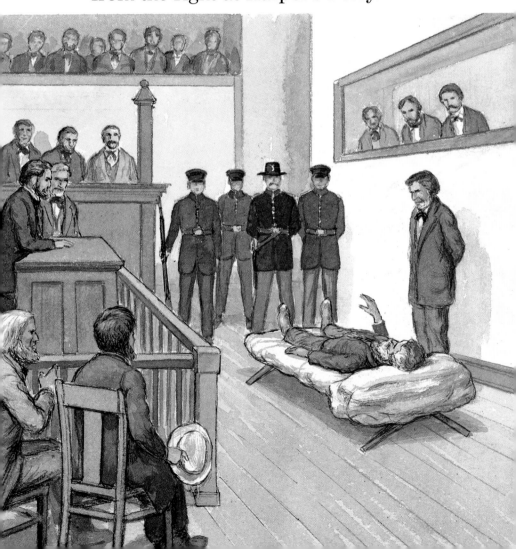

John spoke angrily.

Shouldn't everyone in the United States
be free and equal?

Yes, he had led his men
into Harper's Ferry.

He had broken the law.

But there was a more important law,
he said.

Slavery was against the law of the Bible.

He had followed that law.

The court decided quickly.

John had killed people and acted
against the United States government.
He must die.

John was hanged on December 2, 1859.

Later, six of his men were hanged, too.

Most slaveowners still believed
slavery was right.
More and more Northerners said
it was wrong.
The slaves worked and suffered.
The anger between
the North and the South grew.
Many people decided
that John had been right.
Words would not end slavery.

In 1860, Abraham Lincoln
was elected president.
Lincoln was from the North.
He was against slavery.
Over the next few months,
the states of the South
left the United States.
They made their own country.

President Lincoln wanted to keep
the United States together.
In 1861, the Civil War began
between the North and the South.
It lasted four years.
Over half a million soldiers died.
So did thousands of others.

The North won the war.
The Southern states returned
to the United States.
Over three million slaves
gained their freedom.
But John had been right
when he said slavery would bring
a long and terrible war.

46

Afterword

John Brown broke many laws. He even killed people. He thought it was the only way to end slavery. Some people agreed with him. Others called him a criminal. People still disagree about John Brown. What do you think?

John Brown would have been glad to learn that slavery ended with the Civil War. But after the Civil War, former slaves still faced hunger and poverty. They could not own land, and many could not find work. In the South and in the North, African Americans were treated unfairly.

The fight against racism continues two hundred years after John Brown's birth. Until the 1960s, some states separated black people and white people in stores, on buses, and in schools. Since then, the laws have been changed to say that people of all races must be treated equally in schools, jobs, and public places. But in many ways, racism still divides white people and black people. John Brown's fight to end slavery was just one early step on the long road to equality for African Americans.

Important Dates

1800—John Brown was born on May 9 in Torrington, Connecticut.

1805—Family moved to Hudson Township, Ohio

1812–1814—Saw beating of young slave boy. (The exact date of this event is unknown.)

1818—Built his own tannery

1820—Married Dianthe Lusk

1821—Birth of John Brown Jr., the first of Brown's twenty children

1825—Moved to Randolph, Pennsylvania, and built new tannery

1832—Death of Dianthe Brown

1833—Married Mary Anne Day

1837—Pledged his life to ending slavery

1846—Opened wool business in Springfield, Massachusetts

1847—Met Frederick Douglass and shared secret plan

1849—Wool business failed; moved to African-American community in New Elba, New York

1855—Traveled to the Kansas Territory to work against slavery

1856—In Kansas, led raid against proslavery settlement; five men died

1859—Led raid on Harper's Ferry, Virginia; caught and put on trial; hanged on December 2, 1859